JAMES BOND

Published by
WISE PUBLICATIONS
14-15 Berners Street, London W1T 3LJ, UK.

Exclusive Distributors:
MUSIC SALES LIMITED
Distribution Centre, Newmarket Road,
Bury St Edmunds, Suffolk IP33 3YB, UK.
MUSIC SALES LIMITED
Units 3-4, 17 Willfox Street, Condell Park,
NSW 2200, Australia.

Order No. AM1006060
ISBN: 978-1-78038-877-9
This book © Copyright 2013 Wise Publications,
a division of Music Sales Limited.

Compiled and edited by Jenni Norey.
New music arrangements by Derek Jones.
Music processed by Paul Ewers Music Design.
Cover designed by Michael Bell Design.
Cover photographs courtesy of Photofest.
Printed in the EU.

Your guarantee of quality:
As publishers, we strive to produce every book to
the highest commercial standards.
This book has been carefully designed to minimise awkward
page turns and to make playing from it a real pleasure.
Particular care has been given to specifying acid-free,
neutral-sized paper made from pulps which have not
been elemental chlorine bleached.
This pulp is from farmed sustainable forests and was
produced with special regard for the environment.
Throughout, the printing and binding have been
planned to ensure a sturdy, attractive publication which
should give years of enjoyment.
If your copy fails to meet our high standards,
please inform us and we will gladly replace it.

www.musicsales.com

THE ULTIMATE MUSIC COLLECTION
JAMES BOND
FEATURING MUSIC FROM ALL 23 FILMS

PIANO
VOICE
GUITAR

WISE PUBLICATIONS
part of The Music Sales Group

London / New York / Paris / Sydney / Copenhagen / Berlin / Madrid / Hong Kong / Tokyo

THE JAMES BOND THEME 8
DR. NO

FROM RUSSIA WITH LOVE 12
FROM RUSSIA WITH LOVE

007 THEME 16
FROM RUSSIA WITH LOVE

GOLDFINGER 22
GOLDFINGER

THUNDERBALL 27
THUNDERBALL

YOU ONLY LIVE TWICE 32
YOU ONLY LIVE TWICE

ON HER MAJESTY'S SECRET SERVICE 37
ON HER MAJESTY'S SECRET SERVICE

WE HAVE ALL THE TIME IN THE WORLD 41
ON HER MAJESTY'S SECRET SERVICE

DIAMONDS ARE FOREVER 46
DIAMONDS ARE FOREVER

LIVE AND LET DIE 52
LIVE AND LET DIE

THE MAN WITH THE GOLDEN GUN 56
THE MAN WITH THE GOLDEN GUN

NOBODY DOES IT BETTER 62
THE SPY WHO LOVED ME

MOONRAKER 66
MOONRAKER

FOR YOUR EYES ONLY 70
FOR YOUR EYES ONLY

ALL TIME HIGH 75
OCTOPUSSY

A VIEW TO A KILL 80
A VIEW TO A KILL

THE LIVING DAYLIGHTS 87
THE LIVING DAYLIGHTS

LICENCE TO KILL 94
LICENCE TO KILL

GOLDENEYE 103
GOLDENEYE

TOMORROW NEVER DIES 110
TOMORROW NEVER DIES

THE WORLD IS NOT ENOUGH 117
THE WORLD IS NOT ENOUGH

DIE ANOTHER DAY 123
DIE ANOTHER DAY

YOU KNOW MY NAME 133
CASINO ROYALE

ANOTHER WAY TO DIE 139
QUANTUM OF SOLACE

SKYFALL 147
SKYFALL

THE CONNERY YEARS: 1962 - 1967

Once upon a time James Bond was simply the hero of Ian Fleming's special agent adventure novels and short stories. The character caught the imagination of readers previously accustomed to bluff and basically decent English spy heroes because Bond, by contrast, incorporated some of Fleming's own tastes which included snobbery, misogyny and sadism. Fleming added touches of these to the standard ruthlessness necessary for the 007 job in order to suggest that Bond was an elite killer with taste. His Bond really belonged to the 1950s but kept going on the page until the mid-1960s, before which time the question as to who would play him when the books inevitably became films had already been answered.

Thomas Sean Connery was a young Scottish actor with a handful of so-so films under his belt when, in 1962, he secured the role of James Bond in the first film of the Bond series, *Dr. No*. Already demonstrating his career-long inability to employ any accent other than his own, the Scot struck some as an odd choice to play the quintessential English hero. However, he looked good, moved well and was able to suggest a latent capacity for violence — probably because his youthful brushes with Edinburgh gangsters meant he actually had one. He would appear in half a dozen of the Bond movies for Eon Productions (a.k.a. the 'official' Bond films) and one 'unofficial' film in 1983.

Dr. No arrived with much media fanfare and quickly established an armoury of storytelling mannerisms that would survive for half a century: glib puns to sum up an assassination or a sexual conquest, outrageous stunts, implausible lethal gadgets, improbably customised classic cars and,

most evocative of all, Monty Norman's 'James Bond Theme'. The famous riff became Bond's signature tune, indispensable to more or less every subsequent adventure and never to be displaced by whichever theme song accompanied each of the ensuing films. Uniquely, *Dr. No* had no such song (we can safely discount 'Kingston Calypso' which was used for local colour and plot enhancement in the Jamaican-set story, not movie branding purposes).

Sean Connery, aided by the killer guitar riff, a toupee, an ill-advised trilby hat and a bikini-clad Ursula Andress emerging from the sea (she was naked in the book but the film was less daring) made Bond a movie hit from day one. Connery went on to play Bond again in *From Russia with Love*, *Goldfinger*, *Thunderball* and *You Only Live Twice* before attempting to retire from the role. With Eon ever mindful of international distribution, on the way Bond saw off several colourful villains played by well-known foreign actors such as Lotte Lenya, Harold Sakata, Adolfo Celi and Gert Fröbe.

The songs from the Connery period were all written by various combinations of theatre and movie composers working with John Barry who scored the films. With memorable music, a recognisable plot template, elaborate stunts and a growing sense of familiarity, the James Bond franchise was now firmly established. The only element of uncertainty was the question of who could take over from Connery. Would the public warm to a replacement? Or had Connery been just too successful in making the character his own?

DR. NO (1962)

BOND: Sean Connery.

BOND GIRL: Ursula Andress as Honey Rider.

BOND'S CAR: Chevrolet Bel Air convertible.

BOND'S GADGETS: Bookcase transmitter, self-destructive bag and Geiger counter.

SIDE-KICKS: CIA agent Felix Leiter and Quarrel.

VILLAIN: Joseph Wiseman as Dr. Julius No – a brilliant yet evil scientist and radiation expert with crude, bionic hands able to crush metal – aligned with SPECTRE.

SECRET BASE: A nuclear powered fortress in Crab Key, Jamaica.

HENCHMAN OF NOTE: Professor Dent who tries and fails to kill 007 with a poisonous Tarantula.

VILLAIN'S PLOT: Ending the USA's space programme by disrupting rocket tests.

HOW PLOT IS FOILED: Bond poses as a technician to gain entry to Dr. No's Crab Key nuclear reactor where he causes a melt-down to destroy the lair.

HOW VILLAIN IS DEFEATED: Boiled alive in a steaming vat of radioactive water after fighting with Bond – his metal hands were unable to grip the ladder out of the reactor coolant pool.

THE JAMES BOND THEME

Music by Monty Norman

swing

Em⁷

f

ff

9

FROM RUSSIA WITH LOVE (1963)

BOND: Sean Connery.

BOND GIRL: Daniela Bianchi as Tatiana Romanov.

BOND'S CAR: Bentley Mark IV.

BOND'S GADGETS: Q Branch briefcase with tear gas booby trap, bug detector, MI6 bleeper, tape recorder camera and Armalite AR-7 collapsible rifle.

SIDE-KICKS: Agent Nash from Station Y – killed by Red Grant who assumes his identity to get close to Bond.

VILLAIN: Lotte Lenya as Rosa Klebb – former Soviet SMERSH secret service colonel who defected to SPECTRE. Her signature weapon is a poison-tipped, flick knife blade in the toe of her right shoe.

SECRET BASE: None, although the pivotal action takes place on the Orient Express.

HENCHMAN OF NOTE: Red Grant – a stealthy but physically dominating psychopath, proficient with firearms, hand to hand combat and a garrotte wire concealed in his wristwatch.

VILLAIN'S PLOT: Manipulate Bond into stealing the Russian LEKTOR cryptographic decoding device before killing him in revenge for the death of Dr. No. SPECTRE then plan to sell the device back to the Soviets, embarrassing MI6. Klebb sends Red Grant to get close to 007 in order to kill him.

HOW PLOT IS FOILED: Bond dispatches Red Grant on the Orient Express after tricking him into opening his briefcase filled with tear gas and garrotting the assassin with his own watch gadget.

HOW VILLAIN IS DEFEATED: Posing as a maid, Klebb attempts to snatch the LEKTOR device and kill Bond with her poison-tipped knife shoe. Romanov shoots the villain in the chest as 007 blocks her attack with a chair.

FROM RUSSIA WITH LOVE

Words & Music by Lionel Bart

then, I sud - den - ly knew you'd care a - gain. My run - ning a - round is through, I fly to you from Rus - sia with love. From love.

007 THEME

Music by John Barry

18

19

GOLDFINGER (1964)

BOND: Sean Connery.

BOND GIRL: Honor Blackman as femme fatale Pussy Galore, Goldfinger's personal pilot, and Shirley Eaton as Jill Masterson who is killed by being painted gold for being seduced by 007.

BOND'S CAR: Aston Martin DB5 with revolving licence plates, tire slashing spinner hubcaps, passenger ejector seat, rear bulletproof shield, headlight machine guns and smoke and oil slick spray defences.

BOND'S GADGETS: Big Boy and Little Boy homing beacons.

SIDE-KICKS: CIA agent, Felix Leiter.

VILLAIN: Gert Fröbeas as Auric Goldfinger – a gold obsessed master thief who uses his reputation as a legitimate businessman as a front to smuggle and hoard vast quantities of bullion.

SECRET BASE: A facility in Switzerland owned by one of Goldfinger's companies. After infiltrating the plant Bond is captured and strapped to a table with a cutting laser bearing down upon him. This iconic scene features the memorable exchange between the agent and villain:

"Do you expect me to talk?"

"No Mr. Bond, I expect you to die!"

HENCHMAN OF NOTE: Oddjob – Goldfinger's thickset Korean manservant. A lethal assassin, he is resistant to pain and unwaveringly loyal, armed with a signature razor-sharp, metal rimmed bowling hat keen enough to behead stone statues when thrown.

VILLAIN'S PLOT: Operation Grandslam – a plan to detonate a nuclear bomb within Fort Knox to irradiate the USA's gold reserves, rendering them worthless. Goldfinger then plotted to take advantage of the huge increases in gold prices around the world while giving China an upper hand in global politics. In order to stop the US Army from disrupting the plan, Pussy Galore would fly over and drop nerve gas onto the surrounding area.

HOW PLOT IS FOILED: Bond seduces Pussy Galore, convincing her to swap the nerve gas canisters for an inert substance, allowing reinforcements lead by Felix to try and stop Goldfinger. After confronting the villain inside Fort Knox, Bond is incapacitated and handcuffed to the bomb within the vault, along with Oddjob. Bond manages to free himself and electrocute the henchman with a high-voltage cable after his bowler hat weapon becomes lodged in some metal pipes after a misthrow. Bond is then able to defuse the bomb with only 007 seconds remaining.

HOW VILLAIN IS DEFEATED: While attempting to hijack the flight taking Bond to meet the President, Goldfinger is sucked out of the plane after his stray bullet blows out a window within the pressurised cabin, causing rapid decompression.

GOLDFINGER

Words by Leslie Bricusse & Anthony Newley
Music by John Barry

fear   for a gold - en girl___ knows when he's kissed her

it's the kiss of death from Mis - ter Gold - fin - ger.

Pret - ty girl be - ware of this heart of

gold,   this heart is cold.   Gold-en

THUNDERBALL (1965)

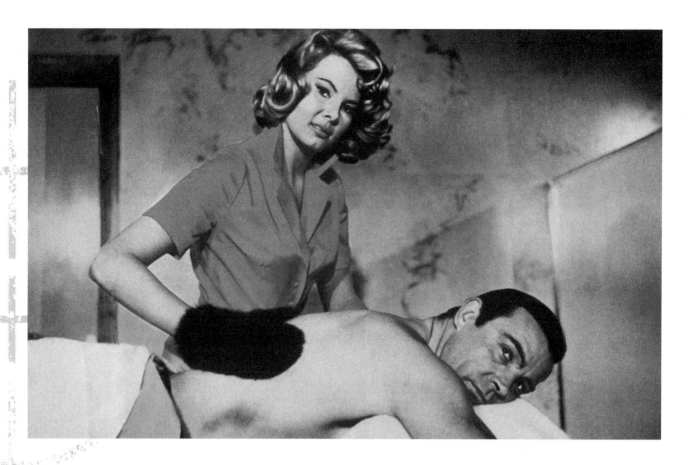

BOND: Sean Connery.

Bond girl: Claudine Auger as Domino Derval – the sister of NATO pilot Francois Derval whose nuclear bomber is brought down as part of SPECTRE's plans. She becomes the mistress of villain Emilio Largo until Bond arrives to foil his scheme.

BOND'S CAR: Aston Martin DB5 with revolving licence plates, tire slashing spinner hubcaps, passenger ejector seat, rear bulletproof shield, headlight machine guns and smoke and oil slick spray defences.

BOND'S GADGETS: Jetpack, underwater breather, underwater jetpack and Geiger counters hidden in Bond's camera and watch.

SIDE-KICKS: CIA agent, Felix Leiter.

VILLAIN: Adolfo Celi as Emilio Largo – Ernst Stavro Blofeld's eye-patch wearing second-in-command and head of SPECTRE's extortion operations.

SECRET BASE: Largo's private estate Palmyra is home to the classic villain's lair feature, the shark pool, and also houses his private yacht, Disco Volante. For a fast getaway the front end can detach to become a high speed hydrofoil.

HENCHMAN OF NOTE: Count Lippe, who attacks Bond at a health spa using a massage machine but instead is thrown into a steamer by 007 and later assassinated by Largo's wife and SPECTRE agent, Fiona Volpe for his failure. After trying to kill Bond herself, Volpe is dispatched in a nightclub after her attempts to lure Bond out into the open for a clean shot backfires when she is shot herself. Largo's right-hand man, Vargas, also attempts to take out the British agent but is impaled by a spear gun.

VILLAIN'S PLOT: Operation Thunderball – stealing two nuclear missiles from a crashed Vulcan bomber and then ransoming the USA and England by threatening to detonate the bombs unless SPECTRE receives £100 million in white flawless uncut diamonds.

HOW PLOT IS FOILED: With the help of the US Coast Guard, Bond defeats Largo's men in an underwater battle before boarding the Disco Volante to confront the villain and secure the warheads. Defecting SPECTRE nuclear scientist Professor Kutze aids Bond by removing the bombs fuses and throwing them into the ocean.

HOW VILLAIN IS DEFEATED: Facing off on the bridge of the Disco Volante, Domino shoots Largo with a speargun, sending him toppling onto the hydrofoil's controls. The ship accelerates and crashes onto rocks before exploding with Largo on board.

THUNDERBALL

Words by Don Black
Music by John Barry

1. He_____ al - ways runs_____ while oth - ers walk._____
2. He_____ knows the mean - ing of suc - cess._____

YOU ONLY LIVE TWICE (1967)

BOND: Sean Connery.

Bond girl: Mie Hama and Akiko Wakabayashi as Japanese Secret Service agents, Kissy Suzuki and Aki. Kissy marries Bond in a mock ceremony to keep him under cover during his mission in Japan as they work together to foil SPECTRE's plot. Aki dies after inadvertently swallowing poison meant for 007 in her sleep.

BOND'S CAR: Toyota 2000GT Open-Top convertible, owned by Aki, who picks up and saves 007 from being assassinated outside a chemical plant before roaring off into an short but intense car chase into the Japanese countryside. Eventually, Aki calls in a Japanese Secret Service helicopter with a powerful electro-magnet attached, literally pulling the chase car off the road, dumping them in the sea.

BOND'S GADGETS: Little Nellie – a heavily armed Gyrocopter that fits into a briefcase when disassembled – and mini-rocket cigarettes.

SIDE-KICKS: Tiger Tanaka – Bond's contact in the Japanese Secret Service who later trains 007 in the ways of the Ninja and leads the attack on SPECTRE's base.

VILLAIN: Donald Pleasance as Ernst Stavro Blofeld – the mastermind behind SPECTRE. This is the first film in which we see the face of Bond's arch-nemesis.

SECRET BASE: A hidden space rocket launch facility located within a hollowed out volcano somewhere in the Sea of Japan. The base houses a piranha pool used by Blofeld to execute and make examples of failed operatives.

HENCHMAN OF NOTE: Mr. Osato, a Japanese industrialist in league with Blofeld who attempts to remove Bond by dripping poison down a string as he sleeps but kills Aki by mistake. He also sends his secretary Helga Brandt to kill Bond by trapping him in the seat of a sabotaged plane. Blofeld's imposing bodyguard Hans attempts to throw Bond into the pool of piranhas after 007 foils his master's plot, but is instead flipped into the water and devoured.

VILLAIN'S PLOT: To push the USA and the Soviet Union towards World War III by hijacking their experimental space craft using a space rocket able to capture other craft and take them back to SPECTRE's base codenamed Bird 01.

HOW PLOT IS FOILED: After being trained in the way of the Ninja, 007 locates and infiltrates SPECTRE's volcano hideout, using the mini-rocket cigarettes to help Kissy, Tiger and the Japanese Secret Service storm the facility. Bond then triggers Bird 01's self-destruct before it can envelope another space craft and trigger nuclear war.

HOW VILLAIN IS DEFEATED: Watching Bond foil his plans yet again, Blofeld escapes, but not before reactivating the dormant volcano to destroy the base with Bond and his allies inside. Thankfully, Bond, Kissy and Tiger, along with the surviving troops of the Japanese Secret Service's ninja platoon, are able to get out just in time.

YOU ONLY LIVE TWICE

Words by Leslie Bricusse
Music by John Barry

TWO BONDS: 1968 - 1971

The choice of Australian model George Lazenby to take over from Connery in 1968 was widely deemed a failure at the time although his sole Bond film, *On Her Majesty's Secret Service* (1969), has undergone something of a re-evaluation over the years. Lazenby's performance too has been more kindly perceived now that the sequence of films spans half a century and *OHMSS* can be seen in context. The unspoken fear in the late 1960s was that Bond was going out of fashion, a male chauvinist throwback that the spirit of the Swinging Sixties had made irrelevant. Connery's withdrawal had already associated Lazenby with that perceived decline and Lazenby himself also felt that Bond was getting a bit passé, which was why he never chose to play Bond again despite having a seven-film contract.

OHMSS also changed the Bond musical habits by using two themes — a John Barry orchestral piece named for the film and a wistful Hal David song performed by Louis Armstrong, 'We Have All The Time In The World', which was referred to as the film's 'secondary' theme.

In the background deals were being done concerning the future of the Bond films and it was in a spirit of some commercial nervousness that

the next one, *Diamonds Are Forever* (1971), was proposed. Wanting a stabilising presence at any price the producers lured Connery back with one last big payday — so big that it caused the special effects budget to be slashed, with noticeable results. Even Connery thought that at 41 he was too old, noting that Bond should be in his early 30s, but the producers got what they paid for insofar as the film was commercially successful. Even so several critics were now starting to tire of some of the more camp elements that in the case of *Diamonds Are Forever* they perceived as a desperate bid to enliven a routine melodrama.

On the music front the John Barry/Don Black title song was entrusted to Shirley Bassey who could always be relied upon to inject drama into a number whether it needed it or not. The result here was a happy one and her version is well remembered by audiences who might have trouble recalling exactly what the film itself was about or who on earth thought it was still acceptable in 1971 to have one of the Bond girls called Plenty O'Toole. James Bond on the cinema screen was still in danger of drifting out of step with public taste and, what was more, next time there would definitely be no Connery on hand to steady the ship.

ON HER MAJESTY'S SECRET SERVICE (1969)

BOND: George Lazenby.

BOND GIRL: Diana Rigg as Teresa di Vincezo. Known to her friends as Tracy, she is the daughter of Marc-Ange Draco, head of the Union Course crime syndicate. After preventing her from committing suicide on a Portuguese beach, Bond falls for di Vincezo, and they eventually marry.

BOND'S CAR: A seemingly normal Aston Martin DBS.

BOND'S GADGETS: Q Branch safe cracker and compact two-way radio.

SIDE-KICKS: Marc-Ange Draco – father of Tracy, and head of the Union Course crime syndicate. Offers Bond a one million pound dowry to marry his daughter while also providing the resources and men to storm and destroy Blofeld's base.

VILLAIN: Telly Savalas as Ernst Stavro Blofeld, who has undergone plastic surgery following his escape in Japan to take on the physical characteristics of the de Bleuchamp family. He uses the title of Count de Bleuchamp as a cover.

SECRET BASE: Piz Gloria – an allergy clinic in the Swiss Alps, used by Blofeld as a front for his brainwashing scheme.

HENCHMAN OF NOTE: Irma Bunt – responsible for supervising operations at Blofeld's clinic. Bunt kills Bond's new wife in revenge for his destruction of the facility and SPECTRE's plans.

VILLAIN'S PLOT: Blackmailing the world with Virus Omega – a biological weapon able to cause mass extinction of plant and animal species, including humans. Blofeld's plan was to spread Virus Omega throughout the world using ten beautiful women, his Angels of Death, brainwashed by the SPECTRE mastermind at his base in the Swiss Alps. Blofeld's demands include a complete pardon as well as official recognition of his title as Count de Bleuchamp.

HOW PLOT IS FOILED: After taking on the guise of Sir Hilary Bray, Bond registers as a patient at Piz Gloria, uncovering Blofeld's plot. With the help of Draco, he destroys the clinic before the plan can come to pass.

HOW VILLAIN IS DEFEATED: Blofeld once again escapes Bond, but gains revenge driving the car from which Bunt fires the shot that kills Teresa.

ON HER MAJESTY'S SECRET SERVICE

Music by John Barry

WE HAVE ALL THE TIME IN THE WORLD

Words by Hal David
Music by John Barry

44

DIAMONDS ARE FOREVER (1971)

BOND: Sean Connery.

BOND GIRL: Jill St. John as diamond smuggler Tiffany Case and Lana Wood as Plenty O'Toole, a beautiful casino patron on the lookout for a high rolling date.

BOND'S CAR: Not a Bond car as such, but 007 does commandeer a moon buggy to make an unlikely off-road getaway.

BOND'S GADGETS: A grappling hook gun, fake fingerprints and vocal algorithm recorder.

SIDE-KICKS: After assuming the identity of smuggler Peter Franks, Bond is able to bring Tiffany Case on-side with his mission. Felix Leiter is yet again on hand to assist 007 in his assignment.

VILLAIN: Charles Gray as Ernst Stavro Blofeld. After chasing the SPECTRE mastermind to Egypt on a mission to avenge the murder of his wife, 007 watches his foe supposedly die in a mud pit at a facility where SPECTRE had been working on a project to create duplicate copies of their chief. However, it soon becomes clear that Bond's satisfaction over Blofeld's demise may have been somewhat premature as the mastermind is again uncovered as the man manipulating world events from the shadows. Blofeld hijacks the business empire of reclusive billionaire, Willard Whyte using his resources and identity as a front and cover for his plot.

SECRET BASE: The Whyte Tectronics research and development facility in the Nevada desert, Willard Whyte's penthouse suite at the Whyte House casino (used by Blofeld as a personal hideout), and a Pacific oil rig used as a control platform to carry out SPECTRE's latest plan.

HENCHMAN OF NOTE: Mr Wint and Mr Kidd.

VILLAIN'S PLOT: Siphoning off a supply of high-quality diamonds from South Africa to create a Refraction Laser Satellite orbital dooms day weapon able to destroy targets on Earth with incredible power and accuracy. To demonstrate the threat posed by his latest weapon, Blofeld destroys American and Chinese missiles and a Russian submarine before blackmailing the USA by aiming its sights on Washington DC.

HOW PLOT IS FOILED: After discovering the whereabouts of Blofeld's oil rig base, Bond alerts Felix and the US Marines who attack the platform to disable the satellite control room.

HOW VILLAIN IS DEFEATED: Blofeld yet again tries to escape 007 by climbing into a personal Bathosub pod. Before the miniature escape submarine can be launched by crane however, Bond grabs the controls, using the suspended capsule containing the villain as a wrecking ball to smash open the fortified satellite control room. As the oil rig explodes, Blofeld is assumed to be dead.

DIAMONDS ARE FOREVER

Words by Don Black
Music by John Barry

47

THE ROGER MOORE YEARS: 1973-1985

Choosing Roger Moore to play Bond signalled a more light-hearted approach. Moore had many times demonstrated his limited but engaging style of acting in a variety of TV roles — *Ivanhoe*, *Maverick*, *The Persuaders* and most impressively in the long-running series *The Saint*. As a film actor Moore had fared unevenly on both sides of the Atlantic and the downside of all this experience was that he was already 46 by the time he began playing Bond and pushing 58 by the time he gave his last performance in the role. Still he made himself at home as 007 even if by the end of his tenure he seemed to require a stunt double for almost everything except the close-ups.

His first appearance as Bond was in *Live And Let Die*, and the film was scored by George Martin rather than John Barry (who was unavailable), and featured Paul and Linda McCartney's version of its theme song, for the first time adding a rock flavour to a Bond song.

Reviews of *Live And Let Die* were mixed and doubts were expressed about everything from its racial attitudes to Moore's lightweight performance. Even so Moore would become the longest-serving

Bond actor, spending twelve years in the role, making seven films in all. During that period Bond was usually portrayed as a mature, slightly louche playboy usually armed with little more than some implausible exploding gadget from Q's toy box and the quizzically raised eyebrow that became the actor's trademark.

Roger Moore soldiered on through *The Man With The Golden Gun* (song featuring Lulu); *The Spy Who Loved Me* (Carly Simon singing 'Nobody Does It Better' the first Bond song not to share the film title); *Moonraker* (Shirley Bassey again); *For Your Eyes Only* (Sheena Easton who also makes a fleeting appearance on screen); *Octopussy* ('All Time High' sung by Rita Coolidge); and finally *A View To A Kill* (Duran Duran).

At this point Moore was retired from the films and, ever the self-deprecator, later admitted "I was only about four hundred years too old for the part". His successor would not only be younger but also more threatening and facially much closer to the early illustrations of Fleming's rather vulpine hero.

LIVE AND LET DIE (1973)

BOND: Roger Moore.

Bond girl: Jane Seymour as Solitaire, a Tarot card reading seer who serves as the film's villain until 007 leads her to distraction.

BOND'S CAR: A rundown double-decker bus used by Bond and Solitaire to make a getaway across the Caribbean island of San Monique.

BOND'S GADGETS: Q Branch shark gun with pressurised air rounds, a Rolex watch featuring a powerful electromagnet and cutting bezel, and a hang glider with signalling light.

SIDE-KICKS: CIA agent Felix Leiter, local Louisiana lawman JW Pepper and Quarrel Jnr, the son of Bond's ally from Dr. No.

VILLAIN: Yaphet Kotto as Dr. Kananga/Mr. Big – The corrupt Prime Minister of San Monique who also doubles as a major drug lord in Harlem and New Orleans.

SECRET BASE: A large poppy plantation on San Monique with nearby underground lair built beneath a voodoo cemetery. Kananga also uses the Fillet of Soul restaurant chain as hideouts and distribution centres across the USA.

HENCHMAN OF NOTE: Tee Hee, Mr Big's formidable smiling enforcer equipped with a powerful mechanical crushing claw for a hand; Whisper, a portly, powerful wrestler who tries to take down Bond both with his strength and a poisonous snake; and Baron Samedi, a seemingly immortal embodiment of the mythical Voodoo Loa of cemeteries.

VILLAIN'S PLOT: Flood the USA with free heroin to destroy the competition and profit from the ensuing monopoly.

HOW PLOT IS FOILED: Escaping from a lake of hungry crocodiles, Bond blows up Mr Big's nearby drug processing facility and heads onto the Louisiana waterways for the film's iconic speedboat chase sequence. Later, Bond disrupts a voodoo ceremony taking place above Mr. Big's secret underground base back in San Monique, in which Solitaire is set to be killed. After saving the Tarot card reader from two apparitions of Baron Samedi – who is first shot and then thrown into a coffin full of snakes – he makes his way below ground to confront the villain.

HOW VILLAIN IS DEFEATED: After throwing Mr. Big into his own shark-infested pool trap, Bond forces a Q Branch compressed air pellet into his mouth, exploding him. Tee Hee is later dispatched by 007 on a train to New Orleans. After locking up his mechanical arm by cutting its control wires, the henchman is thrown out of the carriage window.

LIVE AND LET DIE

Words & Music by Paul & Linda McCartney

do it well,_ you got-ta give the oth-er fel-low hell!_____

THE MAN WITH THE GOLDEN GUN (1974)

BOND: Roger Moore.

BOND GIRL: Brit Ekland as Mary Goodnight, an official at MI6's Hong Kong field base assigned to assist Bond as required, and Maud Adams as Andrea Anders, mistress of the villain, Francisco Scaramanga, who is killed after helping 007.

BOND'S CAR: An AMC Hornet muscle car acquisitioned from a Bangkok car dealership.

BOND'S GADGETS: A fake nipple used by Bond to impersonate Scaramanga and a Q Branch tracking device.

SIDE-KICKS: Local Louisiana sheriff JW Pepper returns, this time off duty and on holiday in Thailand. Bond acquires the AMC Hornet he's waiting to test drive and the pair pursue 007's foe in one of the film series most iconic chases, featuring the corkscrew bridge jump over a river.

VILLAIN: Christopher Lee as Francisco Scaramanga – a suave, freelance assassin who demands a fee of £1 million per job. Armed with a one-bullet, custom golden gun, he is the world's leading hit man and sees himself as Bond's dark equal and the only man able to kill 007. He has the distinctive birthmark of a superfluous third nipple.

SECRET BASE: Scaramanga's secret island base in the South Chinese Sea, featuring a fun house styled training maze in which he tests his skills and trains against live opponents.

HENCHMAN OF NOTE: Nick Nack – Scaramanga's diminutive French manservant who hires rival assassins in secret to try and remove his master in order to inherit his wealth, assets and private, luxury island. He attempts to kill Bond after Scaramanga's plans are foiled at the end of the film, but is incapacitated in a suitcase and tied to a ship's mast.

VILLAIN'S PLOT: Use the stolen Solex Agitator technology to create a high-power energy cannon weapon and then sell off the invention to the highest bidder.

HOW PLOT IS FOILED: After escaping Bond in a car chase across rural Thailand, Scaramanga and Nick Nack convert their Matador muscle car into a jet plane and fly off to the villain's island with Goodnight trapped in the boot. Using a tracking device, 007 discovers Scaramanga's location and defeats him in a dual. While escaping, Goodnight pushes a guard into the Solex Agitator weapon's cooling vat, destabilising the island and causing it to explode. She escapes with Bond on Scaramanga's Chinese junk yacht.

HOW VILLAIN IS DEFEATED: Upon arriving on Scaramanga's island, Bond is greeted warmly as a respected enemy and challenged to a dual that quickly descends into a chase around the lair's fun house maze. Discovering a training doll replica of himself, Bond takes up position in place of the dummy and is able to kill Scaramanga.

THE MAN WITH THE GOLDEN GUN

Words by Don Black
Music by John Barry

THE SPY WHO LOVED ME (1977)

BOND: Roger Moore.

BOND GIRL: Barbara Bach as Major Anya Amasova, Agent Triple X for the KGB.

BOND'S CAR: Lotus Esprit S1 - fondly referred to as Wet Nellie in tribute to Bond's autogyro from *You Only Live Twice*, this was the iconic amphibious supercar able to convert into a submarine when underwater. Highly armed, the car featured cannons that sprayed cement on pursuing vehicles, headlight machine guns, a missile launcher in its rear deck, mines, an underwater black dye smokescreen, and a torpedo bay in its front grille.

BOND'S GADGETS: A ski pole gun and handheld microfilm reader.

SIDE-KICKS: Major Anya Amasova of the KGB is sent on a parallel investigation to Bond in line with Soviet interests. The KGB and MI6 agree a truce between the two agencies so that their agents can cooperate and pool their resources to fulfil their shared mission.

VILLAIN: Curt Jurgens as Karl Stromberg – an anarchist shipping tycoon and scientist with webbed hands who wants to destroy civilisation and start again in his underwater city.

SECRET BASE: Atlantis, a submersible underwater city, and the Liparus, a giant supertanker fitted with an advanced tracking system and able to capture multiple military submarines and their crew.

HENCHMAN OF NOTE: Jaws – Stromberg's huge and seemingly indestructible juggernaut henchman. Armed with a metal crushing jaw and immense strength, he is almost unstoppable.

VILLAIN'S PLOT: To provoke World War III by destroying New York and Moscow with nuclear-armed Intercontinental Ballistic Missiles stolen from hijacked British, American and Soviet submarines. Stromberg planned to ride out the ensuing nuclear Armageddon underwater, creating a new civilization to rule over below the waves.

HOW PLOT IS FOILED: Bond and Amasova are captured by Liparus. While onboard, Bond is able to escape and free the crews of the three submarines trapped inside the super tanker, igniting a battle for control of the ship before the nuclear missiles can launch. After wiring up the British and Chinese submarines to destroy each other, Bond and the liberated submariners escape aboard the American vessel as the Liparus sinks.

HOW VILLAIN IS DEFEATED: Before the fight aboard the Liparus begins, Stromberg retreats to Atlantis with Amasova to act on his plan. After escaping the super tanker, Bond confronts the villain in his underwater base, dispatching him by turning his table long gun trap against him. Following a struggle with Jaws, who is subdued by being thrown into a shark tank, 007 and Agent Triple X flee Atlantis as the Royal Navy fleet bombards and destroys the amphibious city.

NOBODY DOES IT BETTER

Words by Carole Bayer Sager
Music by Marvin Hamlisch

MOONRAKER (1979)

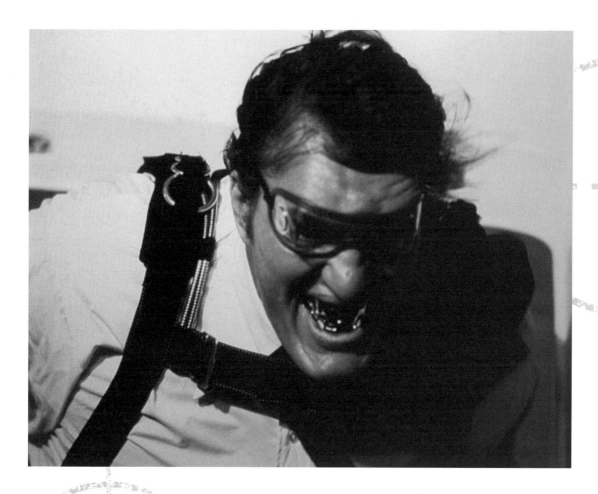

BOND: Roger Moore.

BOND GIRL: Lois Chiles as NASA astronaut, CIA agent and astrophysicist Dr. Holly Goodhead.

BOND'S CAR: Not a car, but while in Venice Bond escapes his assailants on the city's canals by making use of his powered gondola's hidden hovercraft function to leave the water and continue on land.

BOND'S GADGETS: Explosive Seiko watch, wrist-mounted dart gun with cyanide and explosive tip ammunition, safe cracking cigarette case, and a Q Branch power boat equipped with water mines, a heat-seeking torpedo launcher, and motorized hang-glider. *Moonraker* also features a futuristic laser gun used by both Drax's minions and Bond's allies.

SIDE-KICKS: Colonel Scott of the U.S. Space Marines.

VILLAIN: Michael Lonsdale as Sir Hugo Drax – a billionaire industrialist and aerospace magnate whose corporation, Drax Industries, designs and manufactures Moonraker Space Shuttles.

SECRET BASE: An armed space station hidden in orbit around Earth.

HENCHMAN OF NOTE: Jaws – the only henchman to star in more than one Bond film, in *Moonraker*

Jaws was more comical than menacing as Drax's hired enforcer. The metal mouthed man-mountain even switched sides to help 007 at the climax of the film after falling for Dolly, a diminutive female technician on Drax's space station, and realising neither he nor his new love would be included in his master's plans for a purified super race.

VILLAIN'S PLOT: Eradicate humanity with globes of nerve gas launched from space that would leave all other animal and plant life intact. Drax than planned to repopulate the Earth with a new master race of "perfect physical specimens", bred on his space station.

HOW PLOT IS FOILED: Discovering that Drax has a space station hidden in orbit by a jamming system, Bond and Goodhead are able to board one of the Moonraker shuttles set to travel to the station on auto-pilot. Once on board, 007 alerts the U.S. Space Marines to the location of Drax's orbital base, who launch a boarding assault on the facility from their own fleet of shuttles. In an attempt to outmanoeuvre the attack, Drax launches the nerve gas globes which Bond and Goodhead are able to destroy while piloting the villain's own laser-cannon armed shuttle craft.

HOW VILLAIN IS DEFEATED: Before setting off to destroy the globes in his ship, Bond confronts Drax and kills the villain by shooting him with a cyanide-tipped dart and pushing him out of an airlock.

MOONRAKER

Words by Hal David
Music by John Barry

1. Where   are   you?_____   Why do you hide?
2. Where   are   you?_____   When will we meet?

FOR YOUR EYES ONLY (1981)

BOND: Roger Moore.

BOND GIRL: Carole Bouquet as Melina Havelock, the daughter of a murdered marine archaeologist and MI6 agent, and Lynn-Holly Johnson as Bibi Dahl, an Olympic skiing hopeful seeking Kristatos favour and sponsorship.

BOND'S CAR: Two different Lotus Esprit Turbo sports cars – a white model with an explosive self-destruct device and a red version used by Bond in the alps.

BOND'S GADGETS: Q Branch Identigraph machine.

SIDE-KICKS: Milos Columbo – an honourable Greek smuggler who traffics precious metals and luxury goods but not illicit substances or drugs. The film's villain attempts to smear Columbo as the man behind his own plot, but Bond discovers his innocence and instead teams up with the black market mogul.

VILLAIN: Julian Glover as Aristotle Kristatos – A suave and sophisticated Greek shipping magnate and hero of World War II, Kristatos is in fact a ruthless drug smuggler in league with the Soviets. He initially convinces Bond that his rival, Milos Columbo, is the villain by turning the evidence against his own activates to incriminate him.

SECRET BASE: St. Cyril's mountain top monastery.

HENCHMAN OF NOTE: Emile Leopold Locque – a freelance killer who acts as the quiet yet sly and vicious hitman accomplice to Kristatos' seedy smuggler persona.

VILLAIN'S PLOT: Retrieving and then selling off the British ATAC system (a device able to control the nation's submarine launching systems) to the Soviets.

HOW PLOT IS FOILED: After discovering that Kristatos has taken the ATAC system to his monastery base, Bond and Columbo attack the retreat, destroying the device by throwing it from the mountain before the Soviet General Anatol Alexis Gogol can claim it. The General, having made his first appearance in *The Spy Who Loved Me*, is already aware of Bond and his history, preventing his men from shooting 007 after watching him destroy the ATAC machine.

HOW VILLAIN IS DEFEATED: In the assault, Columbo kills Kristatos with a throwing knife to the back. Blofeld also makes an appearance at the opening of the film, where Bond disposes of his greatest enemy once and for all. After taking over the remote control helicopter sent by the SPECTRE boss to kill him, Bond manages to pick up the wheelchair-bound super villain and drop him into an industrial chimney.

FOR YOUR EYES ONLY

Words by Michael Leeson
Music by Bill Conti

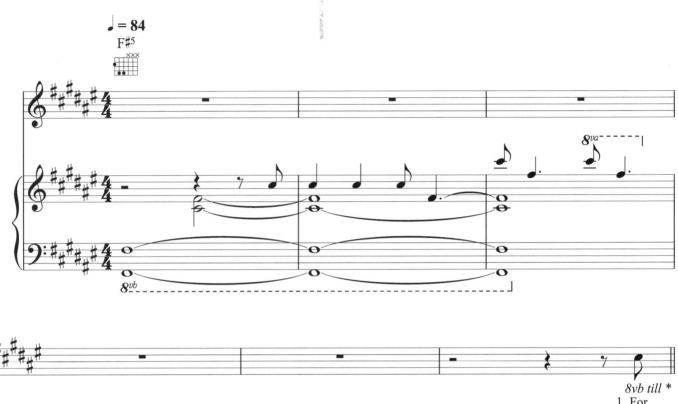

OCTOPUSSY (1983)

BOND: Roger Moore.

BOND GIRL: Maud Adams as Octopussy, a jewel smuggler and head of an international circus.

BOND'S CAR: Alfa Romeo GTV6 – stolen by Bond to escape two Police cars as he races to stop disaster in West Germany. Bond also flies an Acrostar mini jet plane in the movie.

BOND'S GADGETS: Seiko Watch with listening device, fountain pen with corrosive acid and crocodile disguise for travelling down rivers unnoticed.

SIDE-KICKS: Soviet General Anatol Alexis Gogol returns as a moderate and reasoned voice within the Red Army who opposes a plan to invade the West. Gogol's investigation to stop a possible war runs in parallel to Bond's mission.

VILLAIN: Louis Jourdan as Prince Kamel Khan, an exiled royal seeking ever greater riches by collaborating with the worldwide criminal underground; and Steven Berkoff as General Orlov of the Soviet Red Army – a rogue maniac seeking to start World War III.

SECRET BASE: None as such, although Bond does track Khan down at his Monsoon Palace in India and some action takes place within Octopussy's travelling circus.

HENCHMAN OF NOTE: Gobinda, a tall, strong and silent henchman who famously illustrates his fearsome power by crushing a pair of dice with his hands.

VILLAIN'S PLOT: To steal Russian jewels while triggering World War III with a nuclear explosion in West Germany.

HOW PLOT IS FOILED: After preventing a nuclear bomb detonating at one of Octopussy's circus performances at a US Military Base in West Germany, Bond heads to India to lead an attack against Khan's palace.

HOW VILLAIN IS DEFEATED: General Orlov is killed after being mistaken for a deserter as Octopussy's circus train crosses the border from East to West Germany. Prince Khan is dispatched when Bond forces his plane to crash into a cliff.

ALL TIME HIGH

Words by Tim Rice
Music by John Barry

1. All I want-ed was a sweet dis-trac-tion for an hour or two.
2. I don't want to waste a wak-ing mo-ment, I don't want to sleep.

Had no in-ten-tions to do the things we've done.
I'm in so strong and so deep, and so are you.

A VIEW TO A KILL (1985)

BOND: Roger Moore.

BOND GIRL: Tanya Roberts as Stacey Sutton, one-time heiress to an oil company fortune and geologist for the California Department of Oil and Mines. Fiona Fullerton also features as Pola Ivanova, a beautiful KGB agent on a similar mission to Bond focussed on Soviet interests.

BOND'S CAR: The iconic vehicle in *A View To A Kill* isn't a car, but a boat disguised as an iceberg which Bond uses to escape from Russia to Alaska.

BOND'S GADGETS: Q Branch SNOOPER surveillance gadget, ultra-violet device to read pen marks and a credit card with an electronic lock opening mechanism.

SIDE-KICKS: Soviet General Anatol Alexis Gogol is again a silent and in-direct ally for Bond, who rebukes the villain for his plan and its potential effects upon Russia.

VILLAIN: Christopher Walken as Max Zorin – Former KGB operative and product of a secret Nazi fertility experiment that made the few children who survived highly intelligent yet psychopathic. He is the founder and owner of Zorin Industries, a major microchip company.

SECRET BASE: Not so much a secret base as the critical location of Zorin's plot, the villain used his wealth and resources to drill down into an old mine beneath the San Andreas Lake in California.

HENCHMAN OF NOTE: May Day – Zorin's lover and most deadly assassin, blessed with immense physical strength. Played by Grace Jones, May Day defects to Bond's side in order to defeat Zorin after she is betrayed by the villain.

VILLAIN'S PLOT: Detonating a bomb beneath the San Andreas fault causing a double earthquake to flood San Francisco and Silicon Valley, killing millions and allowing Zorin to dominate the world microchip industry.

HOW PLOT IS FOILED: Bond heads into the mine to stop the detonation, confronting May Day at the bombsite. The assassin realises that her lover, Zorin, has abandoned her to die with the bomb as part of his plan and instead decides to use her strength to pull the charge clear of the fault, sacrificing herself to foil the plan.

HOW VILLAIN IS DEFEATED: Enraged by his plan's failure, Zorin attempts to kill Bond while piloting a blimp over San Francisco. The fight comes to a head on top of the Golden Gate Bridge where Zorin attacks 007 with an axe but loses his footing, falling to his death.

A VIEW TO A KILL

Words by John Taylor, Nick Rhodes, Roger Taylor,
Simon Le Bon & Andrew Taylor
Music by John Taylor, John Barry, Nick Rhodes,
Roger Taylor, Simon Le Bon & Andrew Taylor

1. Meet-ing you___ with a view___ to a kill.___
2. Choice for you___ is the view___ to a kill.___

Face to face____ in   se - cret   plac -
Be - tween the shades,____ as - sis - si - na -

- es,   feel   the   chill.
- tions   stand - ing   still.

Night fall____ cov - ers   me.____   But you know____ the
First   crys - tal tears____   fall as snow - flakes

When all we see___ is the view___ to a

kill.

DALTON TAKES OVER: 1987 - 1994

For those who mourned the erosion of Fleming's original James Bond — amoral, tough and dark — Timothy Dalton was a welcome recruit to the role. That was the Bond he brought to life and the first of his two films in the role, *The Living Daylights*, was a very respectable movie. It was also the last Bond film to be scored by John Barry who had been on board for many of the films from the start of the series. Its opening title theme song was performed by the Norwegian group A-ha although a different song, 'If There Was A Man', accompanied the end titles and was sung by Chrissie Hynde.

Timothy Dalton had already enjoyed a distinguished theatrical career and took the Bond role quite seriously, insisting on doing most of his own stunts. Dubbed by purists 'the best Bond ever' his tenure was short, mainly because industry delays postponed the third film he had signed for causing him eventually to pull out, so making his second Bond film, *Licence To Kill*, his last.

Licence To Kill, with a song by Gladys Knight, is also a very creditable film despite evoking the sometimes sadistic spirit of Fleming's Bond in a scene about which even the later Bond movies might have had doubts, where the character played by American model Talisa Soto is whipped. Both in the UK and the US cuts were demanded for 'excessive' and 'realistic' violence.

In the end Dalton can fairly be said to have revived the commercial fortunes of the Bond franchise even though *License To Kill* did rather less well in the US due to its release clashing with some other heavyweight blockbusters. He was a welcome antidote to what many had seen as Roger Moore's physically implausible and over-playful portrayals, and when Dalton said he was pulling out because of the unacceptably long delay over setting up the third film, the search for a replacement began anew. The prime candidate, it turned out, had already been approached before but had been unable to accept due to contractual commitments.

THE LIVING DAYLIGHTS (1987)

BOND: Timothy Dalton.

BOND GIRL: Maryam d'Abo as Kara Milovy, a talented Czechoslovakian Cellist and girlfriend of the film's villain, General Georgi Koskov.

BOND'S CAR: Aston Martin V8 Vantage Volante with extending ski for stable running on ice and snow, spiked tyres, guided attack missiles, wheel-mounted lasers, signal-intercepting radio, rocket booster jump engine and self-destruct capability with hard-wired explosives.

BOND'S GADGETS: Q Branch keychain with stun gas and C4 explosive charge.

SIDE-KICKS: CIA agent Felix Leiter and Kamran Shah, leader of the Mujahideen.

VILLAIN: Joe Don Baker as American arms dealer Brad Whittaker and Jeroen Krabbe as renegade KGB General Georgi Koskov.

SECRET BASE: A secret KGB base in the middle of the Afghanistan dessert and Whittaker's Tangier headquarters.

HENCHMAN OF NOTE: Necros – Whittaker's personal assassin who kills numerous characters throughout the film.

VILLAIN'S PLOT: Selling off stolen diamonds to fund a huge heroin smuggling operation, the proceeds from which would be used to instigate and finance a war between the British and Russian intelligence agencies which Whittaker and Koskov can profit and gain power from.

HOW PLOT IS FOILED: With the help of the Mujahideen, Bond is able to storm the KGB base in Afghanistan and hijack the plane used to smuggle the diamonds and heroin. In a fight with Necros he dumps the drugs over the dessert along with the hit man, depriving the villains of their resources and ruining their scheme.

HOW VILLAIN IS DEFEATED: Bond infiltrates Whittaker's Tangier headquarters, dispatching the arms dealer with his explosive keychain that causes a statue to topple onto the villain, crushing him. The KGB arrive and take Koskov under arrest. He is likely executed.

THE LIVING DAYLIGHTS

Words & Music by John Barry & Pal Waaktaar

1. Hey, driv-er, where we go-ing? I swear my
2. Al-right, hold on tight__ now. It's down,

LICENCE TO KILL (1989)

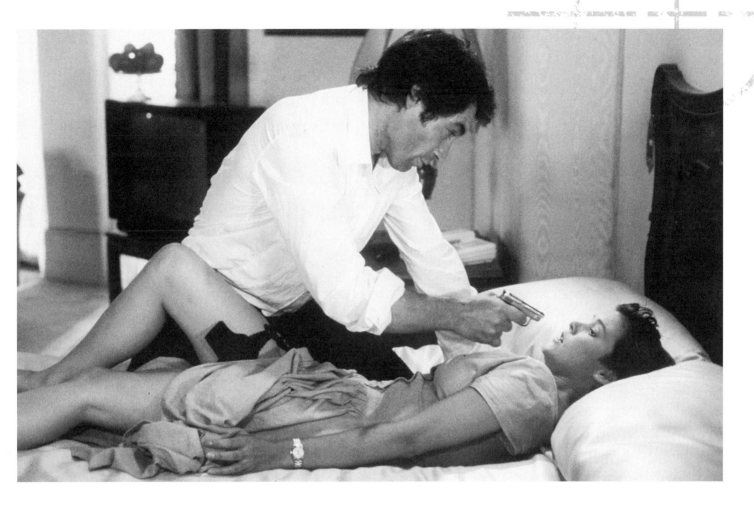

BOND: Timothy Dalton.

BOND GIRL: Carey Lowell as Pam Bouvier, CIA informer and former US army pilot. Bond also runs into Lupe Lamora, played by Talisa Soto, the wife of villain Franz Sanchez.

BOND'S CAR: Bond commandeers an 18-wheeler tanker truck pulling off one of the series great vehicle stunts – balancing the rig on just one of its set of tyres – in a brutish duel down a two lane mountain highway.

BOND'S GADGETS: Plastic explosives disguised as a tube of toothpaste, a camera that converts into a gun only 007 can fire, a laser shooting x-ray photograph camera, an underwater manta ray disguise and a "Felix Lighter", able to produce a light worthy of a small flamethrower.

SIDE-KICKS: Sharkey, a friend of Felix Leiter who owns a boat charting business.

VILLAIN: Robert Davi as Franz Sanchez – a harming but ruthless South American drug lord who feeds Felix Leiter's lower body to his sharks and kills the CIA man's new wife, sending Bond on a mission of vengeance.

SECRET BASE: A drugs laboratory in the Mexican desert.

HENCHMAN OF NOTE: Milton Krest, a business associate of Sanchez and owner of a marina in southern Florida used to smuggle in drugs. Bond convinces Sanchez that Krest is a traitor, causing the drug lord to dispose of him. Dario is Sanchez's bodyguard – a psychopathic, sadistic murderer who enjoys torturing his victims.

VILLAIN'S PLOT: Smuggle cocaine in oil, pumping the drug into the USA through an apparently legitimate pipeline.

HOW PLOT IS FOILED: Resigning from MI6, Bond goes rogue intent on revenge for the crimes committed against Leiter and his wife. Infiltrating Sanchez's inner circle under the persona of a gun for hire, 007's true identity is eventually revealed, forcing his hand into eviscerating the drug lord's empire. He burns down the Mexican drug lab and destroys a convoy of tankers filled with tainted oil.

HOW VILLAIN IS DEFEATED: With his drug smuggling supply chain and distribution network up in flame, a machete-wielding Sanchez clambers onto the back of the convoy's final tanker to confront Bond, which promptly crashes and rolls down a bank. Now soaked in gasoline, Bond uses the Felix Lighter – a best man gift given to him by Felix on the day of his marriage – to set Sanchez alight, sending him stumbling towards a wrecked tanker, causing it to explode.

LICENCE TO KILL

Words & Music by John Barry, Leslie Bricusse, Anthony Newley,
Narada Michael Walden, Walter Afanasieff & Jeffrey Cohen

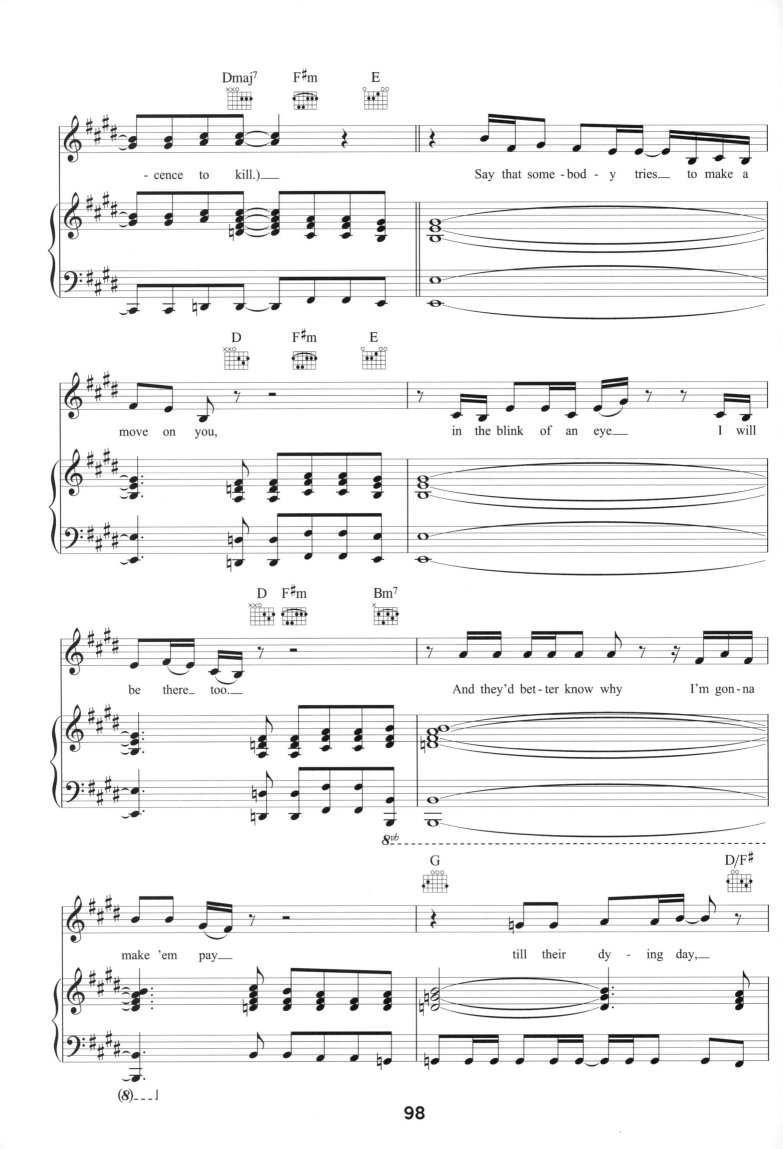

PIERCE BROSNAN: 1995 - 2004

In Pierce Brosnan the producers felt they had found a Bond with a winning blend of looks, credibility and contemporary appeal, less larky than Moore, less intense than Dalton. Brosnan's credentials had been boosted by his successful turn in TV's *Remington Steele* series which ran in the US from 1982 to 1987 with a contract clause that prevented him from taking the Bond role as early as he would have liked. Thus Brosnan was 42 when he finally signed up and 51 when he officially signed off. In between he made four Bond movies which did well although they ended on a comparatively weak note with *Die Another Day* (2002) which got mixed reviews and even some criticism of the impenetrable plot from its star.

The Brosnan years saw the franchise in a holding pattern, still aware that its current Bond was about a decade too old at the outset and that the franchise would now have to keep up with the times if it was to survive. Two years before the end of Brosnan's stint the point was underscored all too graphically by the arrival of the Bourne

films franchise. *The Bourne Identity*'s hero was played by 32-year-old Matt Damon who to all but the most fiercely partisan, was considered a better secret agent action hero than most of the recent Bond incumbents. Damon was helped by the film itself which seemed to strike a much more realistic blend of violent professionalism and human weakness. Still, Bond had the advantage of track record and familiarity, and Brosnan acquitted himself well in *GoldenEye* (1995), *Tomorrow Never Dies* (1997) and *The World Is Not Enough* (1999). The theme song artists were respectively Tina Turner, Sheryl Crow and Garbage. Madonna supplied the song for *Die Another Day*, so setting the seal on a general shift towards pop stars and away from dramatic balladeers. The old question remained: where was the Bond franchise going if it was not to run out of steam? More pressingly, what would the producers be looking for in their next Bond? A blond English actor who was not even born when Sean Connery first stepped into the role, perhaps?

GOLDENEYE (1995)

BOND: Pierce Brosnan.

BOND GIRL: Izabella Scorupco as Natalya Fyodorovna Simonova, a Russian computer programmer at the secret Goldeneye facility in Siberia.

BOND'S CAR: Aston Martin DB5 and BMW Z3. Bond also pilots a T-55 Tank in a memorably destructive chase through St. Petersburg.

BOND'S GADGETS: Explosive grenade ballpoint pen, Omega watch with built-in laser and remote detonator and a belt featuring fireable, high-tensile wire for acrobatic escapes.

SIDE-KICKS: Valentin Zukovsky, an ex-KGB agent turned Russian mafia boss who puts Bond in touch with the Janus syndicate.

VILLAIN: Sean Bean as Alec Trevelyan – Formerly an MI6 operative under the codename of 006, Trevelyan was a close friend and ally of Bond who created the Janus crime syndicate after faking his own death on a mission with 007.

SECRET BASE: A huge satellite dish facility in Cuba hidden beneath a drainable lake.

HENCHMAN OF NOTE: Renegade Russian General Arkady Gregorovich Ouromov who gives

Trevelyan access to the GoldenEye weapon for a share of the profits; former fighter pilot and KGB agent turned Janus syndicate assassin, Xenia Zaragevna Onatopp, likes to kill her targets in compromising positions, crushing their lungs with her thighs; and Boris Ivanovich Grishenko, a brilliant Russian computer programmer able to hack into and control the GoldenEye satellite.

VILLAIN'S PLOT: Use the Russian GoldenEye EMP satellite to disrupt London's banking computers, stealing millions from the British economy electronically while simultaneously erasing any record of the event.

HOW PLOT IS FOILED: Bond and Natalya are able to gain access to the satellite dish facility's control room. While Bond causes mayhem, distracting and fighting Trevelyan and his men with explosions and gunfire, Natalya is able to reprogramme the orbiting satellite to re-enter the Earth's atmosphere and burn up.

HOW VILLAIN IS DEFEATED: While fighting on a platform above the dish, Bond is able to kick Trevelyan off and then let him fall, severely injuring him. As the facility explodes the flaming platform falls and crushes the former 006 agent.

GOLDENEYE

Words & Music by Bono & The Edge

1. See re-flec-tions on the wa-ter, more than dark-ness
2. See him move through smoke and mir-rors. Feel his pre-sence

in the depths.\
in the crowd.

See him sur-face and nev-er a shad-ow;\
Oth-er girls they gath-er 'round him.

on the wind I feel his breath.\
If I had him I would-n't let him out.

Play both times

Guitar chords both times

Gold - en - eye, I've found his weak-ness.\
Gold - en - eye, my lave for leath-er.

Gold - en - eye, he'll\
Gold - en chain break

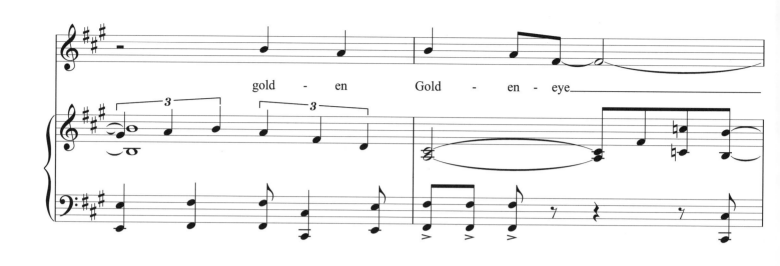

gold - en   Gold - en - eye_____

_____   with a gold - en eye,_____   gold - en - eye.

TOMORROW NEVER DIES (1997)

BOND: Pierce Brosnan.

BOND GIRL: Michelle Yeoh as Wai Lin, a spy for the Chinese People's External Security Force and Terry Hatcher as Paris Carver, Bond's former lover and the wife of the film's antagonist.

BOND'S CAR: A BMW 750iL equipped with missile launchers, caltrops, self-inflating tires and armoured bodywork. The car could also be remotely controlled by Bond's mobile phone. Bond and Wai Lin also make use of a BMW R1200C motorcycle to escape a helicopter, in a chase through the streets of Saigon.

BOND'S GADGETS: Ericsson gadget phone featuring a 20,000 volt shock defence against unauthorised users, finger print scanner, lock pick and flip-open touch surface for remote control of Bond's BMW. An Omega watch is also issued containing a small, detachable detonator charge.

SIDE-KICKS: A highly skilled martial artist and field operative, Wai Lin collaborates with Bond as their parallel investigations for their respective agencies intertwine and overlap.

VILLAIN: Jonathan Pryce as Elliot Carver – a megalomaniac media baron who is constantly seeking to manipulate world events to maximise his profits and influence.

SECRET BASE: A stealth catamaran in the South China Sea armed with a drill-head torpedo able to grind through the hulls of other ships.

HENCHMAN OF NOTE: Mr Stamper – another physically imposing trained killer Bond must outwit, Stamper is a deadly and ruthless assassin skilled in the murderous art of chakra torture.

After Bond kills his mentor, Stamper's assignment to dispose of 007 becomes a personal vendetta of revenge. Henry Gupter is Carver's more technically minded henchman, working in the background to source and reconfigure a stolen GPS encoder.

VILLAIN'S PLOT: Carver aimed to start a war between the UK and China as a marketing device to launch his new worldwide television network while also replacing the current Chinese regime with politicians more sympathetic to his business goals. After using a stolen GPS encoder to send a British Navy frigate off course, Carver's stealth catamaran sinks the ship with its drill torpedo, stealing its on-board cruise missiles. The catamaran then shoots two Chinese fighter jets sent to investigate the incident, while Carver's crew gun down any British survivors using guns loaded with Chinese ammunition.

HOW PLOT IS FOILED: Upon discovering Carver's plan, Bond and Wai Lin locate and board the stealth catamaran. Bond sets off an explosion within the ship, damaging its plating and exposing it to radar, allowing the Royal Navy taskforce in the area to open fire and destroy the vessel. Before the stolen British missiles can be fired, Bond grapples with Stamper, eventually trapping his foe's legs in the launcher's firing mechanism along with some detonators, causing the warheads to explode.

HOW VILLAIN IS DEFEATED: While the ship is under attack, Bond sends Carver's drill-head torpedo into his control room, turning the media mogul into ground mince.

TOMORROW NEVER DIES

Words & Music by Sheryl Crow & Mitchell Froom

1. Darl-ing I'm killed. I'm in a pud-dle on the floor,_
2. Darl-ing you've won. It's no fun. Mar-ti-nis, girls and

D.S. al Coda

Un - til__ that

Coda Db Cm Fm⁶

eyes._____

G⁷ Cm Fm⁶ G⁷

THE WORLD IS NOT ENOUGH (1999)

BOND: Pierce Brosnan.

BOND GIRL: Sophie Marceau as Elektra King, heiress of oil tycoon Sir Robert King, and Denise Richards as Dr Christmas Jones, a Doctor of Atomic Physics overseeing the shutting down of a nuclear test site in Kazakhstan.

BOND'S CAR: BMW Z8 featuring a surface-to-air missile and keychain remote control.

BOND'S GADGETS: Q's fishing boat – built for the unlikely purpose of Q's retirement this compact, high-performance mini speed boat features limited underwater capabilities. Bond is also issued with an Omega watch with grappling hook and flashlight, inflatable bubble ski jacket, and augmented reality eyeglasses for x-ray vision.

SIDE-KICKS: Mafia boss Valentin Zukovsky returns, helping 007 track down his quarry through caucuses. A popular character with fans, Zukovsky eventually sacrifices himself to save Bond's life towards the climax of the film.

VILLAIN: Robert Carlyle as Renard. Born Victor Zokas, Renard is an ex-KGB terrorist who survived being shot in the head by a 00 agent. Instead of killing him instantly, the bullet is slowly travelling through his brain like shrapnel, cutting off his sense as it goes. Consequently this gives Renard incredible strength and endurance due to his inability to feel pain. He previously kidnapped and later fell in love with Elektra King, who is in fact the film's main villain. Renard is determined to see her plan succeed.

SECRET BASE: Istanbul's Maiden's Tower – a discreet islet in the bay of the Bosporus, used by Renard and Elektra as a staging post to enact the final part of their plan.

HENCHMAN OF NOTE: Gabor, Elektra's personal body guard, and Mr Bullion, Zukovsky's right-hand man who betrays his boss and Bond, revealing that his allegiances lie with Renard and his mercenaries.

VILLAIN'S PLOT: Blow up Istanbul by overloading the reactor of a nuclear submarine, rendering the city and its surrounding area highly radioactive. This would hand Elektra King and her new pipeline a monopoly as the only route able to carry oil through the region.

HOW PLOT IS FOILED: After battling through the submarine to the reactor core, Bond and Christmas struggle to stop Renard who is nigh unstoppable in hand-to-hand combat due to his inability to feel pain. Distracting the villain with talk of Elektra, Bond is able to connect a high-pressure hose to the reactor, firing out a rod of plutonium to impale and kill Renard and prevent a meltdown.

HOW VILLAIN IS DEFEATED: Upon landing on the rocky islet of the Maiden's Tower, Bond is capturing and tied into an archaic torture device controlled by Elektra who seeks to kill him slowly and painfully. Zukovsky and his men interrupt however, allowing the Mafia boss to shoot one of the restraints tying Bond to the device with his final breath. Once free, Bond pursues Elektra, killing her after she taunts him and tries to warn Renard of 007's escape.

THE WORLD IS NOT ENOUGH

Words by Don Black
Music by David Arnold

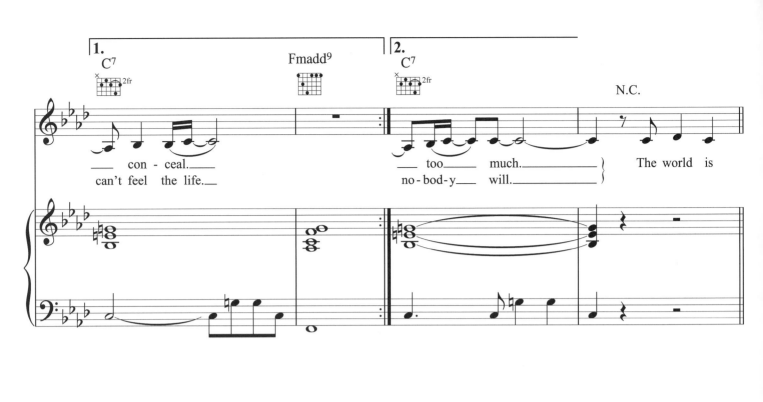

1. C7   Fmadd9   **2.** C7   N.C.

___ con - ceal.___

can't feel the life.___   ___ too___ much.___   no - bod-y___ will.___   The world is

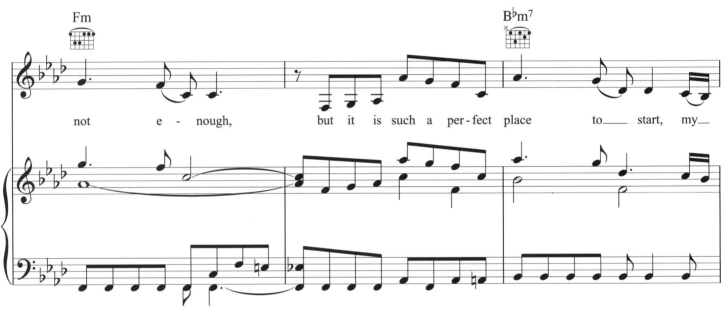

Fm   Bbm7

not   e - nough,   but it is such a per-fect place   to___ start, my___

C   Fm

love.   And if we're strong   e - nough,   to - geth-er we can take the

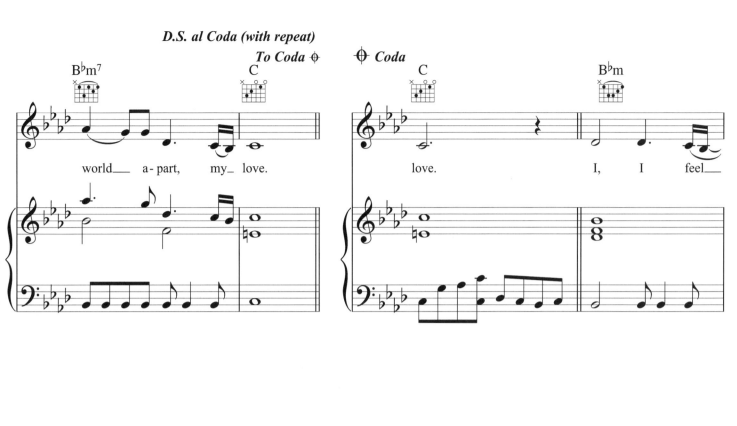

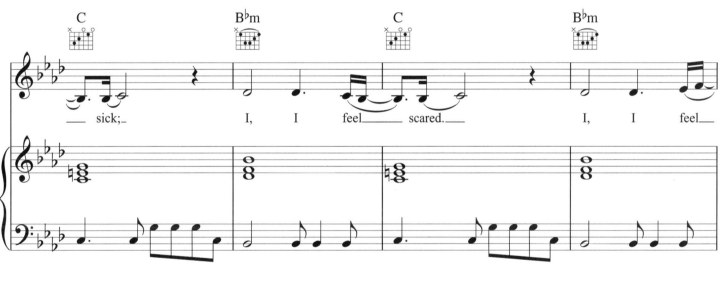

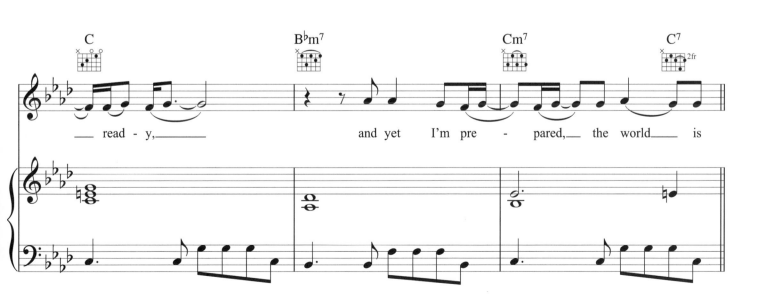

DIE ANOTHER DAY (2002)

BOND: Pierce Brosnan.

BOND GIRL: Halle Berry as Jinx, an NSA agent for the US government, and Rosamund Pike as MI6 operative Miranda Frost, a double agent in the employ of the film's villainous antagonist.

BOND'S CAR: Aston Martin V12 Vanquish – dubbed the Aston Martin Vanish by Q Branch, this hi-tech Bond car was able to turn invisible thanks to an array of micro cameras and projection screens across its bodywork. As well as this adaptive camouflage, the car was also fitted with front-firing rockets, hood-mounted automatic target-seeking shotguns and deployable spikes within its tyres.

BOND'S GADGETS: Single digit glass breaking sonic agitator ring, Omega watch with laser cutter and remote detonator, and a surfboard featuring a hidden compartment for communications equipment, small arms and explosives.

SIDE-KICKS: When her own mission tracking North Korean terrorists crosses path with Bond's, Jinx and 007 decide to pool their resources and team up.

VILLAIN: Toby Stephens and Will Yun Lee as Sir Gustav Graves and Colonel Tan-Gun Moon respectively – a rogue North Korean officer and diamond smuggler who assumes the identity of a suave, sarcastic and arrogant English billionaire by undertaking painful experimental gene-replacement therapy after apparently being killed by Bond. The procedure had the unfortunate side-effect of preventing the villain from sleeping.

SECRET BASE: A grand sculpted ice palace in Iceland.

HENCHMAN OF NOTE: Zao – a North Korean soldier and right-hand man of Colonel Moon, who is scarred by fragments of diamond embedded in his face after a previous run-in with Bond.

VILLAIN'S PLOT: Using an orbital satellite, Icarus, able to capture and focus solar energy into a powerful energy beam, controlled by his own personal power armour interface – able to generate electric shocks as a weapon – Moon planned to cut a path through the mine fields of the Korean demilitarised zone, allowing the North Korean army to invade and conquer South Korea.

HOW PLOT IS FOILED: Aboard the large military cargo plane used by Moon to oversee the battlefield below, the antagonist fires a poor shot, blowing out a large window. Almost everyone on board is sucked out of the plane leaving Bond and Moon to engage in an intense fight which 007 eventually wins, ending the Icarus beam's orbital onslaught.

HOW VILLAIN IS DEFEATED: Armed with his electric shock power armour, Moon grapples with Bond, and seems to hold the upper hand due to his technological advantage. However, Bond is able to turn Moon's armour against him, electric shocking the villain out of a window and into one of the plane's engines, shredding him and his power suit.

DIE ANOTHER DAY

Words & Music by Madonna Ciccone & Mirwais Ahmadzai

guess I'll die an-oth-er day. An-oth-er day.___ I guess I'll die an-oth-er day. An-oth-er day.__ I

guess I'll die an-oth-er day. An-oth-er day.___ I guess I'll die an-oth-er day.

(Spoken:) Siegmund Freud,

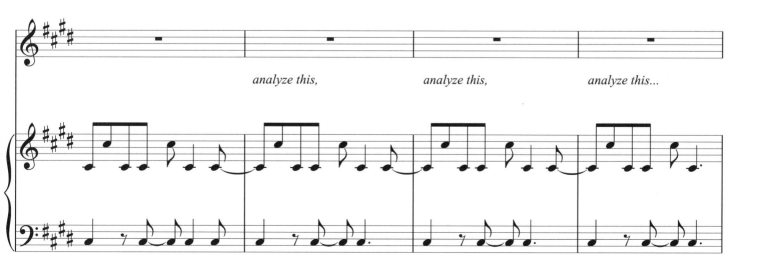

analyze this, analyze this, analyze this...

2. I'm gon-na break___ the cy - cle. I'm gon-na shake___

___ up the sys - tem. I'm gon-na de - stroy my e -

-go. I'm gon - na close___ my bod - y now.___

C#m

I think I'll find an - oth - er way. There's so much more to know.___
For ev -'ry sin, I'll have to pay. A time to work, a time to play.

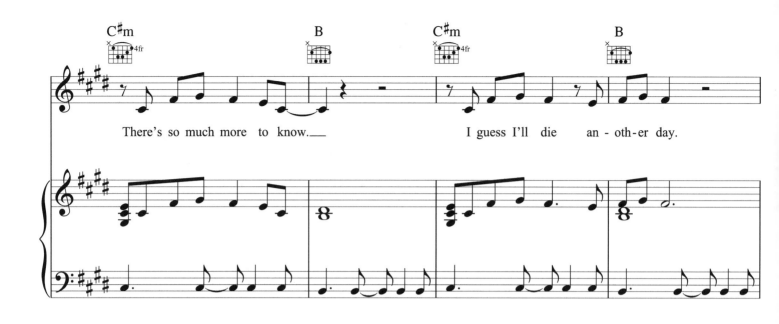

There's so much more to know.___   I guess I'll die an-oth-er day.

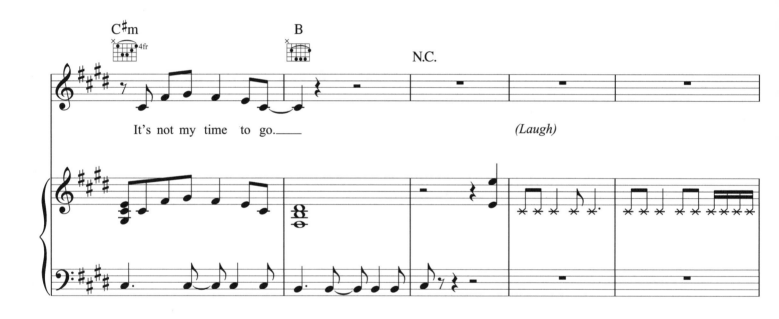

It's not my time to go.___   *(Laugh)*

(Spoken:)   *I need to lay down.*

I guess I'll die an-oth-er day.__ I guess I'll die an-oth-er day.__

__ I guess I'll die an-oth-er day.__ I guess I'll die an-oth-er day.__

__ An-oth - er day.__ An - oth - er day.__ An - oth - er day.__

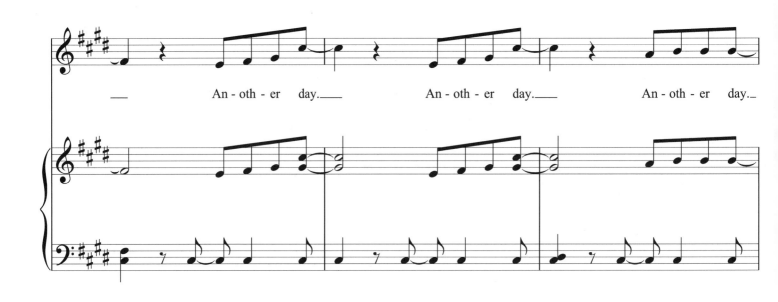

An - oth - er day.___ An - oth - er day.___ An - oth - er day._

N.C.

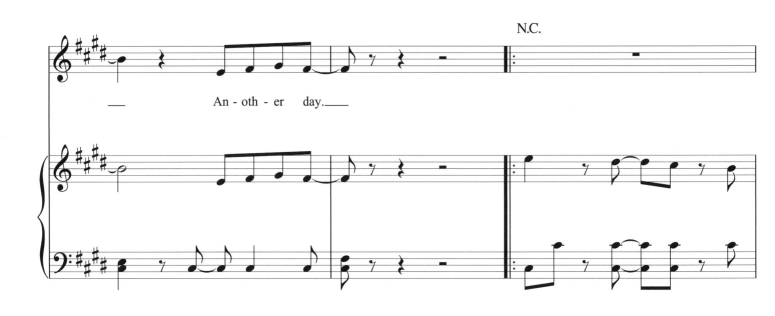

An - oth - er day.___

Repeat ad lib. and fade

DANIEL CRAIG: 2005 - ?

After a Scot, an Australian, two Englishmen and an Irishman the sixth actor to play Bond was once again English. Daniel Craig had built a worthy career on stage and in film without ever looking like a star. Even as he was getting the Bond role he was cast as condemned man Perry Smith in *Infamous*, a film about how Truman Capote interviewed two killers for his book In Cold Blood. The director ruefully recalled how he cast Craig because he was an 'unknown' — just as the international publicity broke about him getting the Bond role.

At 37 Craig brought a muscular presence to the franchise. His first Bond film *Casino Royale* (2006) reinvented the Bond saga by ignoring the chronology of the preceding films and setting it at the start of the agent's career at the point where he acquires his 007 'licence to kill' status. It was essentially the start of a refurbishment of the entire Bond career for new movie audiences.

In *Casino Royale* the music references the plot in that Chris Cornell's song, 'You Know My Name', provides the recurring theme that replaces the traditional James Bond riff which only appears at the end when novice Bond has finally won his spurs. Despite some early press reservations about whether blond and blue-eyed Craig would be suitable for the role, the actor was well-served by the screenplay and by director Martin Campbell. The film was widely deemed a great success.

In 2008 *Quantum of Solace*, loosely based on an Ian Fleming short story of the same baffling title, marked a return to spectacular action and featured a labyrinthine plot rendered more or less incomprehensible by rapid cutting. Jack White and Alicia Keys collaborated on the song 'Another Way To Die' which displaced a potential Mark Ronson/Amy Winehouse contribution that Winehouse was in no shape to record at the time. Critical reception was mixed but the nearest thing to a consensus was that *Quantum of Solace* somehow fell short of its predecessor.

Skyfall (2012) was delayed by yet another of the industry problems that seem to have dogged the Bond films. Eventually it happened with Sam Mendes directing and, almost inevitably, international pop star Adele writing and singing the requisite title song.

Critical consensus concluded that Mendes had this time struck a happy medium between spectacle and humanity and by now everyone seemed to think that Craig had grown into the role. He even won plaudits from crusty partisan commentators like Sir Sean Connery and Sir Roger Moore. Another commentator credited a third knight with being a benign force, citing the dazzling visual style of Christopher Nolan's *The Dark Knight* as an influence. Yet again, the franchise had kept an eye on the competition and found a way to pull in the audiences, most of whom, like Daniel Craig, were not even born when Connery made his first charismatic appearance at the chemin de fer table in *Dr. No* over half a century ago.

CASINO ROYALE (2006)

BOND: Daniel Craig.

BOND GIRL: Eva Green as Vesper Lynd, a British Treasury agent assigned to oversee Bond's mission and use of the fifteen million pound buy-in to enter the Casino Royale high stakes poker tournament.

BOND'S CAR: Aston Martin DBS V12 with a high-tech first aid kit, complete with antidotes and a portable defibrillator, stowed away in the glove compartment.

BOND'S GADGETS: A microchip implant that allows MI6 to track and monitor Bond's whereabouts and condition.

SIDE-KICKS: MI6 informer Rene Mathis is Bond's contact in Montenegro, but his loyalty is questioned by 007 after a series of unfortunate information leaks that could possibly be traced back to him. Felix Leiter returns but not necessarily from the injuries and trauma he suffered at the hands of Franz Sanchez – Casino Royale was partly a reboot of the Bond series and its character's legend.

VILLAIN: Mads Mikkelsen as Le Chiffre – a private banker for international terrorists, he is forced to organise a high stakes poker tournament at Casino Royale in Montenegro in order to recover a client's funds after a failed investment. Jesper Christensen also features as Mr White, a middle-man between Le Chiffre and his clients who can also be relied upon to act as a fixer to clean up any problems should they arise

SECRET BASE: Not a secret base but the main setting of the film; *Casino Royale* in Montenegro.

HENCHMAN OF NOTE: Mollaka, a freelance terrorist skilled in Parkour and Free Running; Carlos, another mercenary hired by Le Chiffre to secure his client's investment; and Le Chiffre's lover who attempts to poison Bond by spiking his drink with Digitalis, a plant-derived toxin able to trigger heart attacks.

VILLAIN'S PLOT: Win enough money to cover the losses incurred with his client's investments in a high-stakes poker tournament.

HOW PLOT IS FOILED: Having overcome a variety of tricks and attempts on his life, Bond wins the tournament and the cash prize, forcing Le Chiffre into a corner as his debtors move in to kill him for his failings.

HOW VILLAIN IS DEFEATED: Le Chiffre is killed by Mr White, who later arranges for Vesper to deliver the prize money to his fellow operatives in a rendezvous in Venice – a deal that would secure Bond's life and the release of her boyfriend, currently being held hostage by Mr White's organisation, Quantum. Bond interrupts however, a move that leads to Vesper's death and a closing scene in which 007 tracks down Mr White to begin a campaign of vengeance against him and his shady underground group.

YOU KNOW MY NAME

Words & Music by David Arnold & Chris Cornell

1. If you take a life do you know what you'll give?
2. If you come inside things will not be the same,

Con pedale

QUANTUM OF SOLACE (2008)

BOND: Daniel Craig.

BOND GIRL: Olga Kurylenko as Camille Montes –
a former Bolivian Secret Agent with a personal
vendetta against the dictatorial General Medrano
who murdered her family.

BOND'S CAR: Aston Martin DBS V12 with a
high-tech first aid kit, complete with antidotes and
a portable defibrillator, stowed away in the glove
compartment – the same car as used in *Casino
Royale*.

BOND'S GADGETS: Sony Ericsson C902 gadget
phone capable of identifying suspects even without
a face-on photograph by compiling multiple images
while logged into the MI6 mainframe.

SIDE-KICKS: CIA agent, Felix Leiter and Rene
Mathis return.

VILLAIN: Mathieu Amalric as Dominic Greene –
an elite member of the secretive Quantum crime
organisation and head of Greene Planet, a front
company supposedly dedicated to ecological
conservation.

SECRET BASE: Perla de las Dunas, a hotel in the
middle of the Bolivian dessert; selected by Greene
as a meeting place out of the way of prying eyes.

HENCHMAN OF NOTE: General Medrano –
a Bolivian general who seeks to restore himself to
power as dictator by cutting a deal with Quantum.
In reality, he is a puppet for Greene and Quantum.

VILLAIN'S PLOT: Monopolise the water supplies of
Bolivia and then exhort the country into paying up
or face severe drought.

HOW PLOT IS FOILED: Once inside Perla de las
Dunas, Bond captures Greene and interrogates
him to reveal everything he knows about Quantum.
Camille kills General Medrano in his hotel room.

HOW VILLAIN IS DEFEATED: After pumping him
for information, 007 abandons him deep in the
harsh Bolivian dessert, leaving him a can of motor
oil to drink. M later informs Bond that Greene was
found dead with a stomach full of oil and two
bullets in his head, indicating that Quantum had
assassinated him for his failings.

ANOTHER WAY TO DIE

Words & Music by Jack White

ta-ble. A man on your side. Or some-one that you think that you can trust. It's just an-oth-er way to

die.

Mm.

Mm.

Vocal ad lib,

die.

N.C.

ta-ble. A man on your side. Or some-one that you think that you can trust. It's just an-oth-er way to

die.___ *Vocal ad lib.*

Shoot 'em up, bang bang.___

Hey! Hey!

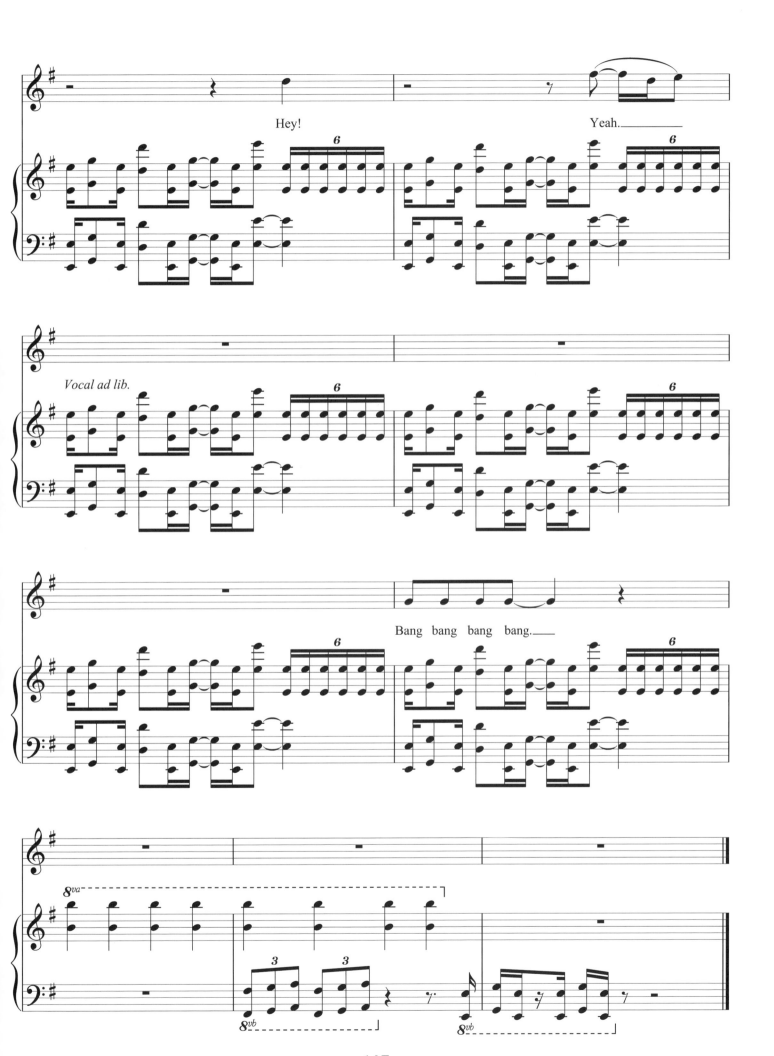

SKYFALL (2012)

BOND: Daniel Craig.

BOND GIRL: Bérénice Marlohe as Séverine, an associate of the villain, Raoul Silva, and Naomie Harris as MI6 Field Agent Eve Moneypenny.

BOND'S CAR: Aston Martin DB5 with headlight machine guns and ejector seat.

BOND'S GADGETS: A simple radio transmitter and palm-print detector to prevent anyone apart from Bond firing his gun.

SIDE-KICKS: Gareth Mallory, Chairman of the Intelligence and Security Committee and Kincade, the elderly gamekeeper of the Bond family's Scottish estate, Skyfall Lodge.

VILLAIN: Javier Bardem as Raoul Silva – MI6 operative turned cyber-terrorist who is able to control or manipulate any system reliant on the internet or computers around the world.

SECRET BASE: A remote island off Macau and former chemical plant which Silva took for himself after hacking in and issuing a warning about a major leak. He runs his near-omnipotent hacking network from the island.

HENCHMAN OF NOTE: Patrice – a mercenary working for Silva as a contract killer. He stole a hard drive containing the identities of all NATO agents currently in the field for his master.

VILLAIN'S PLOT: Kill M in revenge for how she betrayed him when working for MI6.

HOW PLOT IS FOILED: After preventing an attempt on M's life in a government select committee meeting, Bond takes M off the grid by driving to his family's Skyfall estate in the remote Scottish highlands. There he defeats Silva and his cadre of mercenaries with the help of Kincade, M and his Aston Martin DB5.

HOW VILLAIN IS DEFEATED: Having blown up Skyfall in a huge explosion, killing most of Silva's men, Bond interrupts the villain who had tracked a retreating M and Kincade in a local chapel. Bond arrives just in time to kill Silva although M still dies due to a major injury suffered in her earlier escape.

SKYFALL

Words & Music by Paul Epworth & Adele Adkins

Bringing you the words and the music

All the latest music in print... rock & pop plus jazz, blues, country, classical and the best in West End show scores.

- Books to match your favourite CDs.

- Book-and-CD titles with high quality backing tracks for you to play along to. Now you can play guitar or piano with your favourite artist... or simply sing along!

- Audition songbooks with CD backing tracks for both male and female singers for all those with stars in their eyes.

- Can't read music? No problem, you can still play all the hits with our wide range of chord songbooks.

- Check out our range of instrumental tutorial titles, taking you from novice to expert in no time at all!

- Musical show scores include *The Phantom Of The Opera*, *Les Misérables*, *Mamma Mia* and many more hit productions.

- DVD master classes featuring the techniques of top artists.

Visit your local music shop or, in case of difficulty, contact the Marketing Department, Music Sales Limited, Newmarket Road, Bury St Edmunds, Suffolk, IP33 3YB, UK
marketing@musicsales.co.uk